Prayers
with Purpose
for Women

Jackie M. Johnson

BARBOUR
PUBLISHING

© 2010 by Barbour Publishing, Inc.

Compiled by Kathy Shutt.

ISBN 978-1-61626-105-4

Text selections from *Power Prayers for Women*, written and compiled by Jackie M. Johnson, published by Barbour Publishing, Inc.

Published by Barbour Publishing, Inc., P.O. Box 719, Uhrichsville, Ohio 44683 www.barbourbooks.com

Our mission is to publish and distribute inspirational products offering exceptional value and biblical encouragement to the masses.

ECPA Member of the
Evangelical Christian
Publishers Association

Printed in China.

Contents

INTRODUCTION

Prayer Is a Love Connection with God

———— ☺ ————

*H*ow is your love connection? Maybe you talk to God regularly, but you don't feel like you're getting through. Duty has replaced desire, and your quiet time feels dull, routine, or boring. Perhaps, like many people, you want to pray more consistently—but even though your intentions are good, you're too busy and distracted. You want results, but answers take longer than you think they should. And sometimes, when it seems like nothing is happening at all, you wonder if your prayers are working.

When that happens, it's time to get the "power" back in your prayers. How? By connecting and staying connected to the True Source, you could be positively transformed.

Lord, I long to be more connected to You. Teach me to worship You as the True Source of power and love. I adore You like no other. Teach me to pray. Change me, Lord. Transform me so my prayers will be powerful and my life will be fruitful. And may all that I do bring glory to Your name. In Jesus' name. Amen.

MY BIBLE

*The Power of
God's Word*

God's Word Is Truth

───────── ✿ ─────────

*To the Jews who had believed him, Jesus said,
"If you hold to my teaching, you are really my
disciples. Then you will know the truth,
and the truth will set you free."*

JOHN 8:31–32

*T*hank You, Lord, that Your Word
is true. Sometimes it's hard to
discern truth from a lie or from the
half-truths that bombard me daily
from television, radio, magazines, and
popular culture. I want to know the
truth and live it. Help me to look to
Your steady and solid Word, not to this
world, for my life instruction manual. I
thank You that You will never lead me
astray, that You never lie to me, and that
You always keep Your promises.

Light for Understanding

*Your word is a lamp to my
feet and a light for my path.*

PSALM 119:105

*L*ord, Your Word is a lamp in my
darkness—a flashlight on the
path of life that helps me see the way.
Your words enlighten me with wisdom,
insight, and hope, even when I cannot
see where I am going or how things will
turn out. I'm so glad that You know the
right direction. You have gone before
me and are always with me, so I don't
need to be afraid. I choose to follow
Your leading.

Spiritual Refreshment

Listen, O heavens, and I will speak; hear,
O earth, the words of my mouth. Let my
teaching fall like rain and my words
descend like dew, like showers on new grass,
like abundant rain on tender plants. I will
proclaim the name of the LORD. Oh, praise
the greatness of our God!

DEUTERONOMY 32:1–3

*L*ord, I thank You for Your words that speak to my heart and needs. I long to soak in Your teaching and learn more about You. Your life-giving messages are like rain showers on new, green grass. I need not just a sprinkle but a downpour—a soaking, abundant rain in my dry heart! Even though life can be challenging, I will proclaim the name of the Lord and praise the greatness of our God!

Life-Giving Bread

~ ❧ ~

Jesus answered, "It is written: 'Man does not live on bread alone, but on every word that comes from the mouth of God.'"

MATTHEW 4:4

*Y*our Word is my daily nourishment, Lord. Thank You for the Bread of Life You provide every single day. Those words feed and nurture my soul just as eating bread fills me and provides the nutrition I need to live. Without Your words I will fade and die spiritually; with them I am vibrant, energized, and alive! Be my portion, Lord, as I seek You. And not just Your hands and what You give but also Your face, Lord. I desire to know who You really are.

Steady Hope

I wait for the LORD, my soul waits,
and in his word I put my hope.

PSALM 130:5

*L*ord, so many times I am tempted
to think that people or things
will satisfy me. But often they leave
me empty and unfulfilled. Help me to
remember that You are the source of
my hope—not a man or a better job or
a pan of brownies. Those are all good
things, but they will never fully satisfy
me like You do. Forgive me for mis-
placed hope. Help me to put my trust in
You and Your secure, steady, and unfail-
ing love.

God's Word Is Powerful

*For the word of God is living and active.
Sharper than any double-edged sword, it
penetrates even to dividing soul and spirit,
joints and marrow; it judges the thoughts
and attitudes of the heart.*

HEBREWS 4:12

Thank You for Your life-changing words that reveal the true condition of my heart. I can't hide it from You, for You already know everything. But with Your conviction comes repentance and forgiveness. You accept me as I am and give me the grace and power to make real and lasting changes in my life. The Word of God is living and active. That's why it has so much power. I give You my thoughts and attitudes and ask for healing.

Equipped for
Good Work

◎

All Scripture is God-breathed and is useful for
teaching, rebuking, correcting and training in
righteousness, so that the man of God may be
thoroughly equipped for every good work.

2 TIMOTHY 3:16–17

*L*ord, I want to be equipped to
live this life as a Christ-follower.
You breathed Your life into the words
that men put on parchment—which
are now the words of the Bible I read.
Teach me, Lord. Help me to accept
Your rebuke when I need it. Correct
and train me in righteousness so that I
will be ready for whatever life holds for
me today.

The Way to Eternal Life

From infancy you have known the holy Scriptures, which are able to make you wise for salvation through faith in Christ Jesus.

2 Timothy 3:15

*L*ord, I thank You for the signposts You provide in Your Word—for Your directions to heaven. The Bible helps me to be "wise for salvation through faith in Christ Jesus." What a privilege it is to know You through reading about Your Son. He reveals to me what love really is and accepts me just the way I am. You are the Way, the Truth, and the Life, and I choose to follow You.

Wisdom in Interpretation

⊙

Do your best to present yourself to God as one approved, a workman who does not need to be ashamed and who correctly handles the word of truth.

2 TIMOTHY 2:15

*L*ord, I am Your student. Teach me to read Your Word, meditate on it, and apply it to my life. Give me a hunger for spending time with You— and wisdom when I teach Your Word to others. I want to be a person who correctly handles the Word of Truth. I ask the Holy Spirit to enlighten me and give me understanding that I may live right and bring glory to Your name.

To Know God's Will

For this reason, since the day we heard about you, we have not stopped praying for you and asking God to fill you with the knowledge of his will through all spiritual wisdom and understanding.

COLOSSIANS 1:9

Lord, I want to know Your will for my life. Enlighten me with wisdom, discernment, and understanding. I need to know when to stay and when to go, when to speak and when to close my mouth. Fill me with the knowledge of Your best for me—right now and in the future. As I seek to follow You, help me to obediently and joyfully accept Your answers.

MY SALVATION

*The Power of Grace
and Forgiveness*

Prayer for Salvation

——————— ◎ ———————

*If you confess with your mouth, "Jesus is
Lord," and believe in your heart that God
raised him from the dead, you will be saved.*

ROMANS 10:9

*L*ord, I humbly bow before You
now and confess my sins to You.
I am sorry for all of my wrongdoing,
and I ask Your forgiveness. I believe
Jesus is the Son of God and that He died
on a cross and was raised from the dead.
He conquered death so that I might
really live—in power and purpose
here on earth and forever with Him
in heaven. I choose You. Please be my
Savior and my Lord.

Thank You for Saving Me

Thanks be to God for his indescribable gift!

2 CORINTHIANS 9:15

Lord, I thank You for my salvation. I thank You for Your indescribable gift of eternal life and the power to do Your will today. I can hardly fathom how You suffered, yet You did it all for me—for every person on this planet. Mocked and beaten, You bled for my sins. You had victory over death so I could live. You made a way for me, and I am eternally grateful. Thank You, Lord.

A New Beginning

Therefore, if anyone is in Christ, he is a new creation; the old has gone, the new has come!

2 CORINTHIANS 5:17

Lord, now that I am devoted to You heart and soul, I am a new creation. Thank You for washing away my old ways of thinking and behaving and for empowering me to live a new life. Your love changes me! Help me to live this new life with wisdom, making the right choices. Give me the courage to love the way You love. Teach me Your ways as we journey together on this path toward heaven. . .toward home.

Grace Alone

*For it is by grace you have been saved,
through faith—and this not from yourselves,
it is the gift of God—not by works,
so that no one can boast.*

EPHESIANS 2:8–9

*L*ord, You give the best gifts! I receive the love gift of my salvation, knowing that it is by grace that I have been saved, through faith. I didn't do anything to deserve it or earn it. I know my works did not save me, for if they did, then I could boast about it. Instead You saved me by grace so I can now do good works—things You prepared in advance for me to do—to bring glory to Your name.

Only Jesus Saves

"Salvation is found in no one else, for there is no other name under heaven given to men by which we must be saved."

ACTS 4:12

*L*ord, Your Word says that salvation is found in no one else but God's Son, Jesus Christ. Only His name has the power to save. Our society likes to propose alternative ideas and try to convince me that I can find life in other ways—buying more things or finding romance or looking a certain way. Not true! I choose to believe in Jesus, not in other gods, not in other religious philosophies, not in materialism. Thank You for Your power to save.

Forgiven

*"All the prophets testify about him that everyone
who believes in him receives forgiveness
of sins through his name."*

ACTS 10:43

*L*ord, I am grateful for Your
forgiveness. It's Your name, the
name of Jesus, that covers our sins when
we believe in You. As I receive Your
pardon, empower me to have mercy on
others. I thank You that I am forgiven
and free. Please help me to forgive others when they've hurt me, knowing that
You are the One who brings justice.
And please give me the power to forgive
myself, too.

Not Ashamed

I am not ashamed of the gospel, because it is the power of God for the salvation of everyone who believes: first for the Jew, then for the Gentile.

ROMANS 1:16

*L*ord, I am not ashamed of the gospel. Your words have the power to bring salvation to every person who believes. I don't want to hide the light of truth, but instead let it shine from my life so others will see Christ in me. When people ask me about the source of my joy, give me the words to share so they can know You, too. Help me bring glory to You as I stand with courage and strength in the truth.

Words of Life

Simon Peter answered him, "Lord, to whom shall we go? You have the words of eternal life."

John 6:68

*L*ord, You have the words of eternal life that allow us to cross over from death to life, from bondage to freedom, and from misery to peace. Words can be so hurtful at times, but Your words bring life, hope, and healing. You did not come to condemn me but to save me and free me from death. Fill me with Your words of life and hope so I may use them to encourage others.

To Love and Obey

———— ❧ ————

*Like newborn babies, crave pure
spiritual milk, so that by it you may
grow up in your salvation.*

1 PETER 2:2

*L*ord, I want to grow up spiritually. I want to transition from a
newborn baby who drinks only milk to
a more mature believer who craves the
"meat" of deeper things. I want to move
from head knowledge to heart experience with You. I want to know what it
means to enjoy Your presence, not just
to make requests. Step-by-step and day
by day, teach me to follow and learn
Your ways.

MY EMOTIONS

The Power of a Renewed Mind

God and Emotions

❧

"The LORD is slow to anger, abounding in love and forgiving sin and rebellion."

NUMBERS 14:18

*L*ord, what a blessing You are that You have given us such an array of emotions with which to express ourselves. Help me to be more like You—slow to anger and abounding in love. Help me to be a woman who is forgiving. I pray for more discernment, so that in whatever comes my way, I will have the grace to think, speak, and act with a good and godly attitude.

Renewing Your Mind

—— ◎ ——

*Do not conform any longer to the pattern
of this world, but be transformed by the
renewing of your mind. Then you will be able
to test and approve what God's will is—
his good, pleasing and perfect will.*

ROMANS 12:2

*L*ord, sometimes I feel like my
emotions need a makeover.
Renovate me—transform me so I can
be balanced and healthy in my emotions. I ask for Your power to change. I
don't want to be the way I used to be. I
want to be wise and enjoy sound thinking. I want to make good decisions in
how I express myself in my words and
actions. Help me to know Your will and
have a mind that's renewed.

Joy

❧

Our mouths were filled with laughter,
our tongues with songs of joy.

PSALM 126:2

Lord, thank You for the gift of laughter! I thank You for the joy You bring into my life through a child's smile, a luscious peach, a hot bath, and a good night's sleep. Help me remember that when I am "looking up" to You, Lord, I can have a more optimistic outlook and be a more positive person. Keep my eyes on You, not myself or my circumstances, so I can live with a lighter, more joy-filled heart.

Confidence

Have no fear of sudden disaster or of the ruin that overtakes the wicked, for the LORD will be your confidence and will keep your foot from being snared.

PROVERBS 3:25–26

*L*ord, I want to be a more confident woman. I don't want to be afraid of disasters—or just making mistakes. Give me the courage to know that You, Lord, will be my confidence. You keep me from tripping over my tongue and saying the wrong thing. But even when I do, You have the power to make things right again. Thank You for the confidence You give me. Let me walk with my head high because I know who I am in Christ: I am Yours!

Compassion

———— ◎ ————

*Be kind and compassionate to one another,
forgiving each other, just as in
Christ God forgave you.*

EPHESIANS 4:32

Lord, Your compassion for people
is great. You healed the blind,
and You led the people who were lost
like sheep without a shepherd. Create in
me a heart of compassion—enlarge my
vision so I see and help the poor, the sick,
the people who don't know You, and the
people whose concerns You lay upon my
heart. Help me never to be so busy or self-
absorbed that I overlook my family and
friends who may need my assistance.

Stress

Cast your cares on the LORD and he will sustain you; he will never let the righteous fall.

PSALM 55:22

Lord, I can't take one more day of this hectic whirl of life—the traffic, the crying kids, my workload at the office, and everything else I have to handle. Sometimes it just feels like too much! Help me to breathe out my cares, casting them away like line from a fishing rod. But don't let me reel them back in! Here is my burned-out, anxious heart. May Your oceans of love and power replenish me, providing the energy I need to do what You want me to do each day.

Anger

*Get rid of all bitterness, rage and anger,
brawling and slander, along with
every form of malice.*

EPHESIANS 4:31

*L*ord, I am so mad! I am angry, and I need Your help. Why do things have to go so wrong? I need to do something with this heated emotion— and I choose to give You my anger and bitterness, Lord. Help me be rid of it. Redeem the confusion and bring peace to what seems so out of control. Free me from resentment and blame. Show me my part in this conflict as You speak to the heart of my adversary. I need Your healing and peace, Lord.

Sadness

Why are you downcast, O my soul?
Why so disturbed within me? Put your
hope in God, for I will yet praise him.

PSALM 42:5

Lord, I feel so gloomy today. Do
You see my tears? In my sadness,
help me to remember that even when
I'm down, I can choose to put my hope
in You. Instead of telling myself lies
that push me deeper into despair, I can
look to Your truth. Remind me of the
good things You have done in the past. I
choose to praise You. You are my Savior
and my God. May Your love comfort
me now.

Depression

———————— ✺ ————————

He lifted me out of the slimy pit, out of the
mud and mire; he set my feet on a rock and
gave me a firm place to stand. He put a new
song in my mouth, a hymn of praise to our
God. Many will see and fear and put their
trust in the LORD.

PSALM 40:2–3

*L*ord, will You please change the
music of my life from a sad, mi-
nor key to a joy-filled, major key? Give
me a new song to sing, a happier tune!
It's amazing to me that there is no mess
too big for You to fix, no broken life
too shattered for You to restore, and no
loss too great for You to redeem. As You
raise me out of the darkness of my slimy
pit, lifting me from the mud and mire
of my depression to solid emotional
ground, I will praise You.

Foolish Disobedience

At one time we too were foolish, disobe-dient, deceived and enslaved by all kinds of passions and pleasures. We lived in malice and envy, being hated and hating one another. But when the kindness and love of God our Savior appeared, he saved us, not because of righteous things we had done, but because of his mercy. He saved us through the washing of rebirth and renewal by the Holy Spirit.

TITUS 3:3–5

Lord, I have done many foolish things—and I am sorry. I don't want to be disobedient. I have made unwise choices, and I have been deceived and taken captive by the passions and pleasures of the world. Forgive me. Thank You for saving me by Your mercy and a love that's hard to fathom. Sometimes Your kindness startles me—in spite of all I have done wrong. You bring me back to Your good graces. Thank You, gracious Lord.

MY MARRIAGE

The Power of Love

Lord, Change Me

———— ◎ ————

Search me, O God, and know my heart;
test me and know my anxious thoughts.
See if there is any offensive way in me,
and lead me in the way everlasting.

PSALM 139:23–24

*L*ord, look into my life and search my heart. Is there anything hurtful that I have been doing? Remove the sin and selfishness. Help me to stop focusing on how my husband should change. Lord, cleanse *my* heart first. I can't change anyone else, so I ask You to show me what needs to go from my life, what needs to stay, and how I can be right with You. As You do, I pray for greater love and healing in our marriage.

Love Each Other

Above all, love each other deeply, because love covers over a multitude of sins.

1 PETER 4:8

Lord, You are the Author of love. Teach us to love each other deeply, from the heart. I thank You for the love my husband and I share, for the joy and the closeness. When we do something wrong, help each of us to forgive and move past the offense. I pray that our love would be patient and kind, not proud or selfish but seeking each other's good. Protect our love and keep our marriage solid as we put our hope and trust in You.

Deal with Anger

"In your anger do not sin": Do not let the sun go down while you are still angry.

EPHESIANS 4:26

*L*ord, I need Your help in dealing with my anger, whether I am simply annoyed, a little mad, or downright furious. I want to handle this feeling in healthy ways. Help me to process my emotions and not let them fester inside me. Help me to control my temper and talk about what bothers me in calmer ways. Show me how to give my anger to You so I can live in peace with my husband.

Forgive Each Other

Get rid of all bitterness, rage and anger, brawling and slander, along with every form of malice.

EPHESIANS 4:31

Lord, I don't know why forgiveness can sometimes be so hard. We need Your help to get rid of bitterness and anger in our marriage. Help us to build each other up instead of putting each other down—even when it seems we deserve the latter. Teach us grace. Help us to forgive one another and to be kind and compassionate, because we know Christ forgave each of us.

Live in Unity

Be completely humble and gentle;
be patient, bearing with one another in love.
Make every effort to keep the unity of the
Spirit through the bond of peace.

EPHESIANS 4:2–3

*L*ord, I humbly ask that we would be united and strong as a couple. May Your cords of peace, honor, respect, and love hold us together during both the good times and the challenges of our married life. As we become more connected to You, Lord, help us to be closer to each other. Help us to be patient, bearing with one another in love. And help us to live in joyful harmony.

Better Communication

*Instead, speaking the truth in love,
we will in all things grow up into
him who is the Head, that is, Christ.*

EPHESIANS 4:15

*L*ord, I thank You for my wonderful husband. I truly love him, but I need more: I need better communication with him. Help me not to fear asking for what I need emotionally. I pray that You would speak to his heart and that he would learn to listen. Help him to ask me questions about my life and to be present in the conversation. Lord, help us to speak the truth in love and grow closer through better communication.

Revive Us, Lord

*He who refreshes others
will himself be refreshed.*

PROVERBS 11:25

*L*ord, we need a revival in our marriage. I ask that You would restore the connection in our emotions and intimacy. Daily living tires us, and we need time together for true closeness, not just familiarity. I pray that we can rediscover the joy of our love for each other. I want to hold hands and hearts again. Unhurry us, Lord, so we can notice each other and nurture our marriage.

Reignite the Romance

Let him kiss me with the kisses of his mouth—for your love is more delightful than wine.

SONG OF SONGS 1:2

Lord, I ask that You would reignite the romance, the chemistry in my relationship with my husband. The fire of love sometimes dims—and we need it to burn brightly again. Fuel our intimacy with restored affection and passion for each other. Help us to remember the days when we were so eager: I am his! He is mine! And though our relationship has matured, help us always to find fulfillment in this God-ordained expression of love for one another.

Respect Each Other

*Wives, submit to your husbands,
as is fitting in the Lord.*

COLOSSIANS 3:18

*L*ord, I ask that my husband and
I would value each other. As he
loves me, help me to respect him. As
I value him, help him to cherish me.
Teach us to give and to receive in the
ways that are meaningful to each of us.
Help us both to be better listeners and to
seek to understand. Lord, draw us always
closer to You and to each other.

MY CHILDREN

The Power of Encouragement

Love Your Kids

❧

We love because he first loved us.

1 JOHN 4:19

*L*ord, I thank You for loving me and empowering me to love others. Help me to love my kids with words of affirmation and encouragement. Help me to make a priority of giving them my time and attention—to really listen to them so they feel loved and valued. I pray for the wisdom to discipline in love, the energy to play, and the ability to laugh and enjoy my kids. Thank You for my children and Your love for all of us.

Pray for Your Child's Salvation

———— ৩ ————

"I tell you the truth, anyone who will not receive the kingdom of God like a little child will never enter it." And he took the children in his arms, put his hands on them and blessed them.

MARK 10:15–16

*L*ord, I ask and pray in the name and power of Jesus that You would plant a seed in my child's heart to desire You. I pray she would come to know You personally at a young age. Help her to know You as her Savior and Lord and stay on the straight, narrow path to Your kingdom. Give her ears to hear, eyes to see, and a heart to receive Your love gift of salvation. Draw my child to Yourself, I pray.

God's Armor of Protection

———— ◎ ————

*Finally, be strong in the Lord and
in his mighty power. Put on the full
armor of God so that you can take your
stand against the devil's schemes.*

EPHESIANS 6:10–11

*L*ord, I thank You for Your protection of my children. With the
full armor of God, may they be strong in
Your mighty power. Help them to stand
firm with the belt of truth and to put on
the breastplate of righteousness, knowing they are in right standing with you.
May the gospel of peace be like shoes on
their feet. As they take up the shield of
faith, give them the Holy Spirit to fight
for victory over evil. With the helmet of
salvation and the sword of the Spirit—
the actual Word of God—may they be
completely protected.

Teach Them to Pray

We will not hide them from their children; we will tell the next generation the praiseworthy deeds of the LORD, his power, and the wonders he has done. He decreed statutes for Jacob and established the law in Israel, which he commanded our forefathers to teach their children.

PSALM 78:4–5

ord, I pray that You would help me to be a good role model as I teach my kids to pray. As a spiritual coach, empower me to pray *for* them and *with* them. May I provide clear instruction and a consistent example so my children can form good prayer habits. I know that I'm not perfect, but I am submitted to You. I ask that as I follow Your example, Lord, they will follow mine—and be people of prayer.

Teach Them to Obey

Jesus replied, "If anyone loves me,
he will obey my teaching. My Father
will love him, and we will come to him
and make our home with him."

JOHN 14:23

*L*ord, help my kids to love and
obey You—and in doing so to
obey me and my husband. Help them
experience the joy of obedience, knowing that it pleases You and their parents
and leads to blessing. As they learn to
obey, give them cooperative and not
rebellious spirits. And when they fail,
choosing not to obey, please give me
patience and the discernment to know
how to discipline with love.

Prayer for a Newborn

Yet you brought me out of the womb; you made me trust in you even at my mother's breast. From birth I was cast upon you; from my mother's womb you have been my God.

PSALM 22:9–10

*L*ord, I prayed for this child, and You have granted me what I asked. I thank You for the miracle of this new life. I pray Your blessing on our precious baby. I pray for this child's protection and safety. May our baby grow to be strong and healthy in mind, soul, and spirit. Pour Your love and affection into us, and help us to provide that same care and nurture in our child's life. We commit this child to You, Lord. Please bless our baby.

Prayer for Growing Children

———— ☉ ————

But grow in the grace and knowledge of our Lord and Savior Jesus Christ. To him be glory both now and forever! Amen.

2 PETER 3:18

*L*ord, as our children mature, I pray that they would come to know You personally and grow in Your grace and knowledge. May You bring glory to Your name as we help them to grow up. Protect them and keep them in Your tender care as they choose friends and learn to make decisions on their own. Give them a hunger for You. Give them a desire for prayer. Help them to have thankful and giving hearts.

Prayer for Teenagers

"This is what the LORD says to you: 'Do not be afraid or discouraged because of this vast army. For the battle is not yours, but God's.'"

2 CHRONICLES 20:15

Lord, I ask for wisdom and patience through my children's teenage years. As they navigate new waters of growth, replace their confusion with clear thinking. I pray for their self-control and the wisdom not to be swayed by their peers. Give them a passion for You and direction for life. May they be motivated and honest. Help me to connect with my kids at this age and seek to understand their world. I thank You that the battle is not mine to fight but Yours, Lord.

For My Child's Life Mate

❧

Do not arouse or awaken
love until it so desires.

Song of Songs 2:7

*L*ord, I pray for my children's future life partners today. Although they are only kids now, I pray for the spouses who will one day be their husbands or wives. Keep them pure, and help them to wait for love. Bring into my children's lives spouses who are godly, loving, and supportive. I pray for mates who are well suited for my children, so they will seek to serve one another and live in harmony. I pray for Your will and Your timing on these vitally important life decisions.

Prayer for a Rebellious Child

Hear, O heavens! Listen, O earth!
For the LORD has spoken: "I reared
children and brought them up, but
they have rebelled against me."

ISAIAH 1:2

*P*lease, Lord, hear my prayer today for help. I need Your mighty power in my child's life. I pray against disobedience and defiance, and I ask that my rebellious child would return to obey both You and me. O God, I need You. Speak to my prodigal child and have mercy. I pray for restoration and forgiveness as Your gracious love revives this child's heart. Bring my child back to You and to our family again.

MY HOME

*The Power of Harmony
and Hospitality*

A Solid Foundation

❧

*"Therefore everyone who hears these words
of mine and puts them into practice is like a
wise man who built his house on the rock."*

MATTHEW 7:24

*L*ord, I come before You to ask
that You would establish our
home on the solid rock of Your love.
Please be our Cornerstone. I pray that
our family would be rooted in love,
grounded in grace, and rich in respect
for one another. Help us to be a family who reaches up to You, reaches in to
support each other, and reaches out to
the world around us. May we stand firm
as a family built on a foundation of true
faith.

A Place of Love and Respect

───── ☾ ─────

Show proper respect to everyone:
Love the brotherhood of believers,
fear God, honor the king.

1 Peter 2:17

*L*ord, may our home be a place where we show love and respect to each other. Help us to value each member of our family and everyone we welcome into our home. We may not always agree; we may have different opinions. But I pray that we would extend kindness to others and seek to view them as significant, worthy, and valuable. We choose to honor others in our home because we honor You.

Living in Harmony

―――― ⊙ ――――

*They broke bread in their homes and ate
together with glad and sincere hearts.*

ACTS 2:46

*L*ord, may our home be a place
of harmony. Let gladness and
sincerity be hallmarks here as we share
meals together, entertain, live, laugh,
and play together as a family. I pray
against discord and fighting, and I pray
for peace. Give each of us an agreeable
spirit. When the challenges of life come,
help us to love and support each other
with empathy, kindness, and love.

A Safe Place

*My people will live in peaceful
dwelling places, in secure homes,
in undisturbed places of rest.*

ISAIAH 32:18

Lord, I ask that You would be our strong defense and protect our home. May this be a place of safety, comfort, and peace. Guard us from outside forces, and protect us from harmful attacks from within. I pray that the Holy Spirit would put a hedge of protection around our home and family. Lord, we look to You as our refuge, our strength, and our security.

A Family Who Prays Together

---------- ❧ ----------

He and all his family were devout and
God-fearing; he gave generously to those
in need and prayed to God regularly.

ACTS 10:2

*L*ord, I want our family to pray
together more often. We need to
put You first because You are the source
of life—and You are worthy of our first-
fruits of time and attention. Help us
make spending time with You a priority.
I pray that meeting with You together
will draw us closer to You and to each
other. I believe You have so much more
for us. I ask for Your blessing as we seek
to honor You in this way.

Family Celebrations

These days should be remembered and observed in every generation by every family, and in every province and in every city. And these days of Purim should never cease to be celebrated by the Jews, nor should the memory of them die out among their descendants.

ESTHER 9:28

Lord, I thank You for the joy of celebration! Help us to be a family who remembers and gathers together—not just for birthdays and holidays but even to celebrate the little blessings of life. As we laugh and play, eat and drink, challenge and encourage one another, we are thankful for all that You have done in our lives. May we have good memories of our family celebrations.

Managing Your Household

---

*She watches over the affairs of her household
and does not eat the bread of idleness.*

PROVERBS 31:27

Lord, I thank You for the wisdom You give me each day to watch over the affairs of my household. Give me energy to accomplish my work and to keep our home organized and running smoothly. Help me to be a good time manager and to stay centered on Your purposes. I need to get my tasks done, but I also want to nurture and cherish my relationships. Empower me, Lord. Help our home to be a place of order, peace, and enjoyment.

Serve One Another in Love

───── ◎ ─────

You, my brothers, were called to be free. But do not use your freedom to indulge the sinful nature; rather, serve one another in love.

GALATIANS 5:13

*L*ord, teach us how to serve one another. Whether I am preparing dinner, or my daughter is helping her sister rake the yard, or my husband and son are putting out the garbage, may each of us have the right motives. Help us, as we help others, to be loving and encouraging. Let us be more aware of the needs of others—and find delight in making their load easier. Help us to serve with a heart of love and gratitude.

Hospitality

Share with God's people who are in need.
Practice hospitality.

ROMANS 12:13

*L*ord, I thank You for my home.
Show my heart opportunities
to open this home to others. I want to
share what You've provided for me. As I
practice hospitality, may Your love shine
through my life. However my home
compares with others', I thank You for
what I have. I am grateful that Your
Spirit is present here. Give me a generous, open heart, and use my home for
Your good purposes.

MY HEALTH

The Power of Healing and Restoration

For Good Health

"Say to him: 'Long life to you! Good health to you and your household! And good health to all that is yours!'"

1 SAMUEL 25:6

*L*ord, I thank You for my good health. It is a blessing. I pray for Your power to sustain me as I take care of myself—by eating healthy food, drinking enough water, and making movement and exercise a part of my daily life. Give me the self-control and motivation I need to make wise choices to support the health of my mind, my spirit, and my body. Please keep me from injury and illness, and keep me safe, I pray.

For a Positive Attitude

A cheerful look brings joy to the heart, and good news gives health to the bones.

PROVERBS 15:30

Lord, I want a more cheerful out-look on life. I pray for a hope-ful disposition. When I tend toward negativity and cynicism, I know You can heal me. Please help me to live with real joy, not just a pasted-on smile. As I spend more time with You, may Your joy flow through me. And, Lord, may I bring joy to the hearts of others.

Spiritual Health

<hr>

*The LORD is my shepherd, I shall not be
in want. He makes me lie down in green
pastures, he leads me beside quiet waters, he
restores my soul. He guides me in paths of
righteousness for his name's sake. Even though
I walk through the valley of the shadow of
death, I will fear no evil, for you are with me;
your rod and your staff, they comfort me. You
prepare a table before me in the presence of
my enemies. You anoint my head with oil; my
cup overflows. Surely goodness and love will
follow me all the days of my life, and I will
dwell in the house of the LORD forever.*

PSALM 23

Lord, I need Your times of refreshing in my life. Bread of heaven, as
You nourish my body with food, feed my
soul with Your words of comfort and life.
May I be filled with Your healing love,
joy, and goodness. I praise You, Father,
for providing green pastures, places to
relax and unwind in the Spirit. Please still
my heart from distractions and be the
restorer of my soul.

Getting Rid of Stress

*Cast all your anxiety on him
because he cares for you.*

1 PETER 5:7

*L*ord, help me to find relief from
stress in my life. I need to value
rest and make time to relax—and I
need Your power to do so. I cast my
cares on You, my Burden Bearer. Help
me to deal with the toxic, unhealthy
relationships in my life. Give me the
strength to say no when I need better
emotional boundaries. And please help
me find joy again in the things I like to
do—unwinding with music, taking a
walk, calling a friend, or learning a new
hobby. Calm me and renew me, Lord.

Rest for the Weary

———— ◎ ————

*"Come to me, all you who are weary and
burdened, and I will give you rest. Take my
yoke upon you and learn from me, for I am
gentle and humble in heart, and you will find
rest for your souls. For my yoke is easy
and my burden is light."*

Matthew 11:28–30

Lord, I need rest. I am so tired
and worn-out. I pray that I will
sleep well at night. I ask for more energy during the day and a more vibrant
spirit. Lighten my load so I can have
a better balance among my work, my
ministry, and my home life. Replenish
me, Lord. As I unwind in spirit and
body, please fill me with peace and rest.

Eating Right

Go, eat your food with gladness,
and drink your wine with a joyful heart,
for it is now that God favors what you do.

ECCLESIASTES 9:7

*L*ord, I thank You for filling the
earth with a bounty of food.
I praise You for the variety of fruits,
vegetables, proteins, and carbohydrates
You provide for sustaining life. Help me
to make a priority of eating a nutritious
blend of foods, to drink enough water,
and to avoid overindulging in junk
food. I pray for the time to shop and
cook balanced meals. Please help me
find food that is healthy and good-
tasting and the will to eat in moderation.

Keeping Your Mind Active

So then, let us not be like others, who are asleep, but let us be alert and self-controlled.

1 THESSALONIANS 5:6

Lord, I want to keep my mind healthy and active. Give me wisdom regarding what I put into my mind. I need to feed it the right things so I can be alert and self-controlled. Keep me from watching mind-polluting junk on television or at the movies. Open my mind to healthy pursuits that challenge my thinking, grow good thoughts, and help me to be a wiser, godlier person.

Prayer for Healing

―――――――― ⟲ ――――――――

*This was to fulfill what was spoken
through the prophet Isaiah: "He took up
our infirmities and carried our diseases."*

Matthew 8:17

Lord God, my Healer, I ask in the
name of Jesus that You would
relieve my injury or illness today. By
Your wounds, Lord, I am healed. I ask
that You would relieve my pain and
suffering. Show the doctors how to best
help me. Touch me with Your power
and Your presence. I humbly ask You to
make me well. And if You choose not
to, Lord, help me to praise You anyway,
looking for the good purpose You have
in my life. Your will be done, Father.

Living with Pain

Great is the LORD and most worthy of praise; his greatness no one can fathom.

PSALM 145:3

*L*ord, I choose to praise You through this pain. You are great, and there is no one worthy of Your honor and glory. "Heal me, O LORD, and I will be healed; save me and I will be saved, for you are the one I praise" (Jeremiah 17:14). I give You this discomfort, and I ask in the name and power of Jesus that You would take it away. Help me and heal me completely from my hurt. Let my heart ache only for the comfort and healing balm of Your presence.

When Healing Does Not Come

I consider that our present sufferings are not worth comparing with the glory that will be revealed in us. . . . And we know that in all things God works for the good of those who love him, who have been called according to his purpose.

ROMANS 8:18, 28

Lord, I have prayed, and healing hasn't come. It's hard to know why You do not heal when You clearly have the power to do so. Please help me not to focus on my present suffering but to be transformed in my attitude. May I revel in the glory that will be revealed in me through this and, ultimately, when I am with You in heaven. I do not understand, but I choose to praise You anyway. Give me the peace, comfort, and assurance that all things, even this, will work for my good and for Your glory.

MY JOY

The Power of Obedience

Finding Strength

---

*"Go and enjoy choice food and sweet drinks,
and send some to those who have nothing
prepared. This day is sacred to our Lord.
Do not grieve, for the joy of the LORD
is your strength."*

NEHEMIAH 8:10

Lord, I am tired and weary.
Infuse me with life, energy, and
joy again. I thank You for being my
strength and my delight. I don't have to
look to a bowl of ice cream or the com-
pliments of a friend to fill me up on the
inside. Steady and constant, You are my
source; You are the One who fills me.
Sustain me, Lord, with the power of
Your love, so I can live my life refreshed
and renewed.

Joy Despite Trials

Consider it pure joy, my brothers, whenever you face trials of many kinds, because you know that the testing of your faith develops perseverance. Perseverance must finish its work so that you may be mature and complete, not lacking anything. If any of you lacks wisdom, he should ask God, who gives generously to all without finding fault, and it will be given to him.

JAMES 1:2–5

*L*ord, it seems odd to consider trials a joyful thing. But I pray that my challenges in life, these times of testing, will lead me to greater perseverance. May that perseverance finish its work so I will be mature and complete, on my way to wholeness. I ask for wisdom and Your perspective as I seek joy in life's challenges—and the better times that will come my way.

Joyful in Hope

Be joyful in hope, patient in affliction,
faithful in prayer.

ROMANS 12:12

*L*ord, I thank You for giving me
hope. I don't know where I would
be without You. I don't know what the
future holds, but You give me the ability
to be joyful even while I wait—even
when I don't understand. Please help me
to have a positive attitude and live with a
mind-set of patience and courage as You
work Your will in my life. Help me to
remain faithful in prayer, Lord, and fully
committed to You.

Joy in God's Protection

*But let all who take refuge in you be glad;
let them ever sing for joy. Spread your
protection over them, that those who
love your name may rejoice in you.*

PSALM 5:11

Lord, please cover me. Protect
me from my enemies—fear and
doubt, worry and human reasoning. I
try to figure everything out, but I end
up confused and tired. Let me rest in the
comfort of Your love and the safety of
Your protection. Here, abiding in You,
I am secure and I am glad. Spread Your
consolation over me as I rejoice in You.
You are my joy and my protection, Lord.

Real and Lasting Joy

For the kingdom of God is not a matter of eating and drinking, but of righteousness, peace and joy in the Holy Spirit.

ROMANS 14:17

*L*ord, I am so tired of imitations. People pretend to be something they're not. Food is flavored with artificial ingredients. It's hard to tell what is false and what is true anymore. When it comes to joy, I want the real thing. Pour into my life Your genuine and lasting joy. I need more of You, Lord. I pray for righteousness, peace, and joy in the Holy Spirit. Fill me, please.

Finding Joy in God's Presence

"You have made known to me the paths of life;
you will fill me with joy in your presence."

ACTS 2:28

Lord, draw me closer to You. In Your presence is fullness of joy— and I want to be filled. Knowing I am loved by You makes me glad; I cannot imagine life without You. With You there is light; without You, darkness. With You there is pleasure; without You, pain. You care, You comfort, You really listen. Here in Your presence, I am loved, I am renewed, and I am very happy.

Obedience Leads to Joy

─────────── ◎ ───────────

"As the Father has loved me, so have I loved you. Now remain in my love. If you obey my commands, you will remain in my love, just as I have obeyed my Father's commands and remain in his love. I have told you this so that my joy may be in you and that your joy may be complete."

JOHN 15:9–11

Lord, Your Word says that if we obey Your commands, we will remain in Your love. I want to serve You out of an obedient, not a rebellious, heart. Just as Jesus submits to You, Father, I choose to submit to You, too. Obedience leads to a blessing. Empower me, encourage me, and give me the will to want to make right decisions, decisions that lead to a better life and greater joy.

Your Reward Will Come

Therefore, since we are surrounded by such a great cloud of witnesses, let us throw off everything that hinders and the sin that so easily entangles, and let us run with perseverance the race marked out for us. Let us fix our eyes on Jesus, the author and perfecter of our faith, who for the joy set before him endured the cross, scorning its shame, and sat down at the right hand of the throne of God. Consider him who endured such opposition from sinful men, so that you will not grow weary and lose heart.

HEBREWS 12:1–3

*L*ord, sometimes I get worn-out and weary. I work hard; I try to do the right thing. But I lose focus. Help me to fix my eyes on *Your* power, not *my* circumstances. Lift me up, and help me to remember the joy of the reward to come. I pray for perseverance as I consider the joy of the prize: I get to be with You forever in heaven. Free of pain, full of joy. Refresh me with Your truth, O Lord.

The Joy of Knowing Jesus

Restore to me the joy of your salvation and grant me a willing spirit, to sustain me.

PSALM 51:12

Jesus, knowing You brings me joy! I am so glad that I am saved and on my way to heaven. Thank You for the abundant life You provide. I can smile because I know that You love me. I can be positive because You have the power to heal, restore, and revive. Your presence brings me joy—just being with You is such a privilege. You are awesome, and I delight to know You and tell others about You.

MY PEACE

*The Power of
Contentment*

Be a Peacemaker

———— ☙ ————

*"Blessed are the peacemakers,
for they will be called sons of God."*

MATTHEW 5:9

*L*ord, please make me a tool of
Your peace. Instead of the hammer of judgment, let me bring the balm
of love. Instead of bitterness and resentment, help me to quickly forgive. When
doubt misaligns my emotions, level
me with faith. When I cannot find an
answer, let me know Your great hope.
When I cannot see the way, bring Your
light to my darkness. When I am feeling
low, bring me joy. Lord, let me receive
all these things so I can console others
and be a peacemaker. (Inspired by the
prayer of St. Francis of Assisi.)

Jesus, Prince of Peace

For to us a child is born, to us a son is given, and the government will be on his shoulders. And he will be called Wonderful Counselor, Mighty God, Everlasting Father, Prince of Peace.

ISAIAH 9:6

Lord, I thank You that I can have a calm spirit—because You are the Prince of Peace. Your name, Jesus, has the authority to make fear and worry flee. Your name has power! You are called Wonderful Counselor because You freely give wisdom and guidance. You are the Mighty God, the One who made the entire world and keeps it all going. My Everlasting Father, it's Your love and compassion that sustain me. My Prince of Peace, I worship and honor You.

Calm My Anxious Heart

Do not be anxious about anything, but in everything, by prayer and petition, with thanksgiving, present your requests to God. And the peace of God, which transcends all understanding, will guard your hearts and your minds in Christ Jesus.

PHILIPPIANS 4:6–7

*L*ord, I don't want to be anxious about anything, but so often I am. I thank You that You understand. Right now I release my burdens and cares to You. I give You my heavy heart and my flailing emotions. I ask that You calm me, despite all that is happening in my life. As I keep my thoughts, actions, and attitudes centered on Jesus, Your peace comes. I thank You for Your peace that settles on me even when I do not understand.

Finding Contentment

Godliness with contentment is great gain.

1 TIMOTHY 6:6

*L*ord, please help me to find my contentment in You. I don't want to be defined by "stuff"—the things I own or what I do. May my greatest happiness in life be knowing who You are and who I am in Christ. May I treasure the simple things in life, those things that bring me peace. With Your grace I rest secure. Like Mary I choose to sit at Your feet. You, Lord, are my satisfaction.

The Peace That Brings Life

———— ✺ ————

A heart at peace gives life to the body,
but envy rots the bones.

PROVERBS 14:30

*L*ord, I thank You for the peace that restores me mentally, emotionally, and physically. It is the peace that brings wholeness. When my heart is restless, my health suffers. But when I am at peace, You restore my entire body. I can breathe easier, I can relax, and I can smile again because I know everything's going to be all right. You are in control. I thank You that Your peace brings life.

The Wisdom of Peace

⟋

But the wisdom that comes from heaven is first of all pure; then peace-loving, considerate, submissive, full of mercy and good fruit, impartial and sincere. Peacemakers who sow in peace raise a harvest of righteousness.

JAMES 3:17–18

*L*ord, please plant Your wisdom in me like seeds in the soil. Each one is a gift from heaven. Help me cultivate each one and learn to follow Your ways. They are pure, peace-loving, considerate, submissive, full of mercy and good fruit, impartial, and sincere. May I be a person who sows in peace and raises a harvest of righteousness. As I look to Your Word for growth, teach me to meditate on it and apply it to my life.

Where Is Peace Found?

*For the kingdom of God is not a matter of
eating and drinking, but of righteousness,
peace and joy in the Holy Spirit, because
anyone who serves Christ in this way is
pleasing to God and approved by men.*

ROMANS 14:17–18

*L*ord, everyone is looking for peace.
Some travel to other countries or
try alternative philosophies and lifestyles
to find an inner tranquility. Some think
food or wine will satisfy the hole in the
heart that only You can fill. But Your
Word tells us it's not what we eat or drink
that provides lasting satisfaction. May I
find peace and joy in Your Holy Spirit,
Lord. Knowing You, loving You, and
experiencing You is true peace. Thank
You, Lord.

Focus on God,
Not Circumstances

*You will keep in perfect peace him whose
mind is steadfast, because he trusts in you.*

ISAIAH 26:3

*L*ord, so many times it seems
as if a thief is trying to steal
my peace. My circumstances can be
overwhelming—and they shake me up.
I don't want to be robbed of happiness
and emotional stability. I ask that You
would keep me in perfect peace as I
choose to keep my eyes on You rather
than on my problems. Let my mind be
steady, not racing. Let my heart trust
that You will see me through.

Peace Like a River

─────────── ◎ ───────────

*If only you had paid attention to my com-
mands, your peace would have been like a river,
your righteousness like the waves of the sea.*

Isaiah 48:18

Lord, I need Your river of life to
flow through me today. Wash
away my cares, and help me to follow
as I learn to "go with the flow" of Your
will. Still my restless heart with the
grandeur of Your creation. I can imagine myself walking on a sandy shore,
the ocean mist and rhythmic music of
the waves revealing Your splendor. I ap-
preciate all You have made. I thank You
for the peace Your creation brings.

Not as the World Gives

*"Peace I leave with you; my peace I give you.
I do not give to you as the world gives.
Do not let your hearts be troubled
and do not be afraid."*

JOHN 14:27

*L*ord, Your peace is unlike any-thing that the world offers. I don't need to upgrade to a new model every year—there's no "Peace 5.0" to download. I have the only version I need when I have Your peace, whether that's a calm tranquility, a quiet stillness, or the inner knowledge that everything's going to be all right. I value my right standing with You and the harmony that brings to my relationships. Your peace is real and lasting, never to be taken away.

MY FEARS

The Power of Faith

No Doubt

But when he asks, he must believe and not doubt, because he who doubts is like a wave of the sea, blown and tossed by the wind.

JAMES 1:6

*L*ord, rescue me from my sea of doubt and fear. I have lived with uncertainty and suspicion for too long. I don't want to be like an ocean wave that is blown and tossed by the wind. I ask that You would quiet my stormy emotions and help me believe that You will take care of me. When I'm tempted to be cynical, help me choose to step away from fear and closer to faith.

Light in My Darkness

*The LORD is my light and my salvation—
whom shall I fear? The LORD is the strong-
hold of my life—of whom shall I be afraid?*

PSALM 27:1

*L*ord, often I am afraid. In the
dark, challenging times of my
life I can't always see the way. I don't
know what to do or where to go. But
You are light! I thank You that You can
see in the dark—the darkness is as light
to You—so I don't have to be afraid.
When my enemies try to ruin my life,
they don't stand a chance, Lord. You
save me. No matter what happens, I
will be confident in You.

God Strengthens You

———— ☺ ————

"So do not fear, for I am with you; do not be dismayed, for I am your God. I will strengthen you and help you; I will uphold you with my righteous right hand."

Isaiah 41:10

*L*ord, I need Your strength in me. Stronger than steel, Your character is so solid I don't have to be afraid. You are with me—and that means everything. I can have joy because of Your joy in me. With Your righteous right hand You help me, deliver me, and uphold me. As You take my hand and say, "Do not fear. I will help you," I smile in gratitude and thanks.

God Will Save You

Strengthen the feeble hands, steady the knees that give way; say to those with fearful hearts, "Be strong, do not fear; your God will come, he will come with vengeance; with divine retribution he will come to save you."

ISAIAH 35:3–4

_L_ord, steady me. Strengthen the emotional muscle of my heart so that I am not so fearful all the time. I want to be stronger. I want to have more faith. I choose to believe in the One who knows everything and has the power to change hearts and lives. My God will come. My God will save me and take care of the ones who have hurt me. I watch and pray for Your justice, Lord.

God Is More Than Able

*I know whom I have believed, and am
convinced that he is able to guard what
I have entrusted to him for that day.*

2 TIMOTHY 1:12

ord, I am so grateful that I know
You—and I am learning more
about Your character every day. You are
holy and sovereign and righteous and
just. You are loving and faithful and
always good. When I know the One
I believe and have a strong conviction
that He is willing and able to help me,
I can have more peace. You *want* to
help me! My God will take care of me.
Thank You, Lord.

God's Power to Conquer Fear

"But I have raised you up for this very purpose, that I might show you my power and that my name might be proclaimed in all the earth."

EXODUS 9:16

*L*ord, You never give in to defeat. You are a strong conqueror of sin and evil. I need Your authority and influence to muscle fear out of my life. You called Moses to lead the Israelites from slavery to freedom. Lead me from my own personal bondage to walk in freedom and peace. Show Your power in my life, and let Your name be lifted up. You get the credit, Lord—let everyone know what You have done to change me.

Freedom from Fear

*You did not receive a spirit that makes
you a slave again to fear, but you received
the Spirit of sonship. And by him we cry,
"Abba, Father."*

ROMANS 8:15

*L*ord, I ask in the name of Jesus
that You would deliver me from
fear. Let doubt be gone! Let cynicism
flee! Instead of a spirit that makes me a
slave again to fear, I have received the
Spirit of sonship—or daughtership in
my case. Abba, Father, rescue me from
terror, dread, and the fearful anticipation
of things that scare me. I cannot do this
on my own. Deliver me, Lord, to Your
freedom and peace.

God Is Your Comfort

*He restores my soul. He guides me in paths of
righteousness for his name's sake. Even though
I walk through the valley of the shadow of
death, I will fear no evil, for you are with me;
your rod and your staff, they comfort me.*

PSALM 23:3–4

*L*ord, there is none like You.
When I am sad, You are my
comfort. Your calm presence restores
my soul. Your words are cool, refreshing water to my spirit. Despite my
confusion, You guide me in paths of
righteousness, and it's all for Your glory.
Even when I feel like I'm lost in a dark
valley, I will not be afraid—for You are
with me. Your gentle strength and Your
divine authority comfort me.

Safe in Danger

For in the day of trouble he will keep me safe in his dwelling; he will hide me in the shelter of his tabernacle and set me high upon a rock.

PSALM 27:5

*L*ord, I need Your protection. Keep me safe in Your dwelling place. Hide me from my enemies in Your secure shelter. Comfort me with Your warm blanket of peace and love. I am safe with You, and in Your protection—in Your presence—I can move from fearful to fearless, from timid to trusting. Here, Lord, I am safe from harm.

MY WORK

The Power of Influence

Thank You for My Work

It is good to praise the LORD and make music to your name, O Most High.

PSALM 92:1

Lord, I praise You and thank You for my work. You are full of goodness and grace. My occupation gives me the ability to shape lives and influence people in positive ways every day, whether it's taking time for teachable moments with my kids or being a listening ear for a coworker. Thank You for my job and the ability to be a "missionary" wherever my feet tread. Season my words so that others may taste and see that my Lord is good.

God's Will for My Work Life

"For I know the plans I have for you,"
declares the LORD, "plans to prosper you
and not to harm you, plans to give
you hope and a future."

JEREMIAH 29:11

*L*ord, I need wisdom and guidance in my work life. Please show me if this is the vocation I should be in right now or if I should change and find another job. I want to use my skills and abilities, as well as my interests, for Your glory. When I feel underutilized and yearn for something more, reveal to me where I can best serve in the coming season of my life.

Working with Excellence

---

*Commit to the LORD whatever you do,
and your plans will succeed.*

PROVERBS 16:3

*L*ord, You give me work to do
every day. Whether it's at home
or in the marketplace, help me to honor
You in my efforts. I don't want to be
satisfied with mediocrity. I ask that You
would empower me to do superior work
and bring glory to Your name. Help me
not to be a clock-watcher or time waster
but to find fulfillment in the tasks
before me. Help me to be a woman of
excellence, integrity, and good ideas in
my place of employment.

Getting Along with Coworkers

How good and pleasant it is when brothers live together in unity!

PSALM 133:1

*L*ord, I thank You for the people with whom I work and spend time every day. Help us to nurture an environment of peace and harmony. When people get along, it's a good thing! Give us respect for each other and patience to deal with disagreements. Even though we're all busy, help us to have more connectedness and unity so we can be more efficient and find more enjoyment in our work. Lord, please bless me and my relationships in the workplace.

Responding Well to Criticism

A fool shows his annoyance at once, but a prudent man overlooks an insult. A truthful witness gives honest testimony, but a false witness tells lies. Reckless words pierce like a sword, but the tongue of the wise brings healing.

PROVERBS 12:16–18

Lord, I don't like being criticized. I ask for a calm spirit when others make cutting remarks. Please give me insight to know if what is said is true—and if I need to make changes in my life. If not, Lord, I ask You to heal my heart from these verbal barbs. Please give me patience and discernment to keep my cool and not lash out in retaliation. Please bring our relationship through this criticism.

Reducing Stress

———————— ☺ ————————

Do not be anxious about anything, but in everything, by prayer and petition, with thanksgiving, present your requests to God.

PHILIPPIANS 4:6

Lord, I have so much to do—please help me! Deadlines and details swirl around me like a swarm of bees. I feel intense pressure with my heavy workload. Help me to do what needs to be done each day so I can stop worrying and rest well at night. I give You my anxiety and stress—I release it all to You, Lord. As Your peace covers me—the peace that passes all understanding—may it guard my heart and mind in Christ Jesus. I rest in the comfort of Your love.

Servant-Style Leadership

"Not so with you. Instead, whoever wants to become great among you must be your servant, and whoever wants to be first must be your slave—just as the Son of Man did not come to be served, but to serve, and to give his life as a ransom for many."

MATTHEW 20:26–28

*L*ord, teach me to be a leader by being a servant. Your ways are so unlike the ways of the world. Strange as it may seem, You say that "whoever wants to become great among you must be your servant." Help me to be more like Christ, as He did not come to be served but to serve. Remove pride, selfishness, and arrogance from my life—and supply me, Lord, with humility and a heart that serves.

The Value of Motherhood

*The wise woman builds her house,
but with her own hands the foolish
one tears hers down.*

PROVERBS 14:1

*L*ord, I thank You that You value
the calling of motherhood. As I
work to serve my family and build our
house into a home, I pray for wisdom,
endurance, energy, and joy. Help me to
know that raising children is a significant
and high honor. I don't have to be in an
office to be significant. Thank You for the
privilege of building strong and lasting
values into my children.

A Good Attitude

—————— ☉ ——————

*"I have told you these things, so that
in me you may have peace. In this world
you will have trouble. But take heart!
I have overcome the world."*

JOHN 16:33

*L*ord, I lift up to You my attitude
at work. As I go about my day,
may I have a positive outlook and a
helpful spirit. Help me to be encouraging and supportive to others. Amid the
activity—and sometimes the chaos—
may my heart be at peace as the Holy
Spirit strengthens and empowers me. Be
the Lord of my emotions as I seek to serve
You in my vocation.

MY FINANCES

The Power of
Wise Stewardship

Biblical Perspective
on Money

———————— ☙ ————————

*Now it is required that those who have been
given a trust must prove faithful.*

1 CORINTHIANS 4:2

Lord, I am thankful for the financial resources with which You have blessed me. I want to be a good steward, a wise manager, of the resources You have entrusted to me. Help me to save and spend with discernment and to give to others in need. Help me to find balance—not be a hoarder or an out-of-control spender. Give me a godly view of money and guidance to use it in ways that will honor You.

Spending Wisely

For the love of money is a root of all kinds of evil. Some people, eager for money, have wandered from the faith and pierced themselves with many griefs.

1 Timothy 6:10

Lord, You are the One who gives wisdom—and I ask that You would give me the discernment I need to spend money sensibly. I need money to pay my bills and meet my obligations. I know from Your Word that money itself is not evil; it's the love of money—greed—that makes us wander from the faith. Help me to spend the money You provide not in self-indulgence but in good judgment.

Saving and Investing

*In the house of the wise are stores
of choice food and oil, but a foolish
man devours all he has.*

PROVERBS 21:20

*L*ord, I pray that You would lead
me to wise financial advice.
When I look, help me to find a trusted
source who can give me direction as to
where to best save and invest my resources. Please provide for my needs today and help me to save for the future.
Help me to be responsible with my
finances as I trust You as my provider.

Joy in Giving

Each man should give what he has decided in his heart to give, not reluctantly or under compulsion, for God loves a cheerful giver.

2 CORINTHIANS 9:7

Lord, I thank You for Your blessings. Whether in plenty or with little, I want to be a cheerful giver. I desire to give from a full heart that serves, not reluctantly or with complaining. I long to see Your money used in ways that will bless others—through my tithing at church, giving to mission organizations, or helping the needy. I choose to give at whatever level I can—and ask You to bless it.

Dealing with Debt

*I call on the LORD in my distress,
and he answers me.*

PSALM 120:1

*L*ord, I need help. My debt is mounting higher and higher; it's getting out of control. Please show me creative ways to pay it off, and help me to save and spend with wisdom. I ask for the resources to pay down my credit cards, loans, and other debts. Show me where I can cut back on spending so I'll have more funds available. Lord, please clean up this mess I've created. Reveal to me the ways I can learn from this and begin again.

Help for a Materialistic Attitude

Keep your lives free from the love of money and be content with what you have, because God has said, "Never will I leave you; never will I forsake you."

HEBREWS 13:5

Lord, at times I'm so affected by this world—I am tempted to want what others have or long for things that I see on television. Change my attitude, Lord. Help me to understand that acquiring more "stuff" won't necessarily make me happy. Being filled with *You* brings true contentment. Teach me the joy and lasting satisfaction that comes from looking solely to You, Lord.

God Will Provide

*"Therefore I tell you, do not worry about your
life, what you will eat or drink; or about
your body, what you will wear. Is not life
more important than food, and the body more
important than clothes? Look at the birds of
the air; they do not sow or reap or store away
in barns, and yet your heavenly Father feeds
them. Are you not much more valuable than
they? Who of you by worrying can add a
single hour to his life?"*

MATTHEW 6:25–27

*L*ord, I thank You for providing for my needs. I give You
my worries and fears—those nagging
thoughts about lacking money for
clothes, food, and the basics of life. You
feed the sparrows in the field, Lord—
You'll certainly help me and my family.
Your resources are limitless—You have
an abundance of blessings. I praise You
for Your goodness, Lord, and the faithfulness of Your provision.

Treasures in Heaven

"Do not store up for yourselves treasures on earth, where moth and rust destroy, and where thieves break in and steal. But store up for yourselves treasures in heaven, where moth and rust do not destroy, and where thieves do not break in and steal. For where your treasure is, there your heart will be also."

Matthew 6:19–21

Lord, You are my true treasure. I value all that You are—holy, wise, loving, and just. You are mighty and powerful, the Giver of life. Help me to take my eyes off *things* as a source of meaning; they may be nice and helpful, but inevitably they fade away. My hope is in You, Lord, and my fortune to come, in heaven.

MY CHURCH

The Power of Worship

Prayer for Good Relationships

———— ❧ ————

"My command is this:
Love each other as I have loved you."

*L*ord, I pray for each member of this church—that we would get along. Despite our variety of backgrounds and opinions, help us to live and worship in harmony. Give us the ability to value and respect our differences. Protect us against divisions, and help us to be like-minded. We all have different gifts, roles, and functions, but we are collectively one body, Lord—Yours. Bind us together with ties of faith and fruitfulness.

Thank You for My Church Family

*Therefore, as we have opportunity, let us
do good to all people, especially to those who
belong to the family of believers.*

GALATIANS 6:10

*L*ord, I thank You for my church
and the people there, my brothers and sisters in Christ. May we grow
together as a "family" of believers as
we learn to love and serve each other.
Although we are different, help us to
respect each other and seek to build
up one another. It is a blessing to have
people to experience life with, both the
good times and the bad. May we be
better connected as we all learn to know
You and love You more.

Prayer for Pastor and His Family

We always thank God, the Father of our Lord Jesus Christ, when we pray for you, because we have heard of your faith in Christ Jesus and of the love you have for all the saints.

COLOSSIANS 1:3–4

Lord, I thank You for our pastor. He is a blessing to our church. I pray that You would enable him with strong leadership skills and wise decision-making abilities. Help him to be a godly man, devoted to seeking and following You. Protect him and his family from the temptations of the world. Though he may have a heavy load, please be His continual refreshment. Help him to guard his time with his family, and keep them strong and loving.

Prayer for a Church's Staff

———— ❧ ————

*On the contrary, we speak as men approved
by God to be entrusted with the gospel.
We are not trying to please men but God,
who tests our hearts.*

1 THESSALONIANS 2:4

*L*ord, I thank You for all the committed people who work on staff at our church. Thank You for their faithful service every day in the offices and on committees. Help them in their daily decisions to serve You and not to seek to please people. May they do their jobs efficiently and well so that all they do builds up the church and furthers Your kingdom.

Prayer for Sunday School, Bible Study, and Small-Group Leaders

The body is a unit, though it is made up of many parts; and though all its parts are many, they form one body. So it is with Christ. For we were all baptized by one Spirit into one body—whether Jews or Greeks, slave or free—and we were all given the one Spirit to drink.

1 Corinthians 12:12–13

*L*ord, I thank You for the faithful servants who teach in our Sunday school, Bible studies, and small groups. Week after week they present the truth from Your Word to help children and adults know You better. Though we all have different functions in the church, we are all one body—and I thank You that You knit us all together in unity. Bless these men and women who serve for Your glory.

Prayer for Church Service Ministries and Volunteers

Therefore I glory in Christ Jesus in my service to God.

ROMANS 15:17

Lord, I praise You that You raise up people to serve the needs of our church. Bless the ones who provide for us as worship leaders, ushers, greeters, sound and media workers, and the entire church ministry team. Bless the kitchen workers, nursery workers, parking lot attendants, ushers, maintenance staff, and others—all the people in front or behind the scenes, Lord, who keep our church running smoothly and well.

Prayer for Revival

"But you will receive power when the Holy Spirit comes on you; and you will be my witnesses in Jerusalem, and in all Judea and Samaria, and to the ends of the earth."

ACTS 1:8

*L*ord, we pray for the Holy Spirit's power to come in a mighty way to each individual who attends our church. As we find personal revival, may it grow to light a mighty fire of passion for God in our church—then spread to our community, our nation, and our world. Please give us a heart to pray for revival and hands that put our faith to action with service to others.

Prayer for Missionaries

Then Jesus came to them and said, "All authority in heaven and on earth has been given to me. Therefore go and make disciples of all nations, baptizing them in the name of the Father and of the Son and of the Holy Spirit, and teaching them to obey everything I have commanded you. And surely I am with you always, to the very end of the age."

MATTHEW 28:18–20

*L*ord, I thank You for our missionaries, both foreign and domestic. Empower them, fill them, and sustain them as they seek to fulfill Your great commission. Give them godly wisdom and good communication as they preach, teach, disciple, and baptize people from all nations. Please meet their needs for a close relationship with You, give them protection and safety, and provide for their financial needs. And, Lord, bless them with emotionally healthy relationships and harmony on their team.

MY MINISTRY

The Power of Reaching Out

Release More Power in My Ministry

―――――― ❧ ――――――

May the God of peace, who through the blood of the eternal covenant brought back from the dead our Lord Jesus, that great Shepherd of the sheep, equip you with everything good for doing his will, and may he work in us what is pleasing to him, through Jesus Christ, to whom be glory for ever and ever. Amen.

HEBREWS 13:20–21

Lord God, I need You. I ask that You would release more of Your power into my life and ministry. God of peace, equip me with everything good to do Your will. Help me to have compassion, integrity, and wise leadership. Work in me what is pleasing to You, Lord. Empower me, enlighten me, and change me so I can be more effective in serving. Let Your name be glorified and honored in all my ministry activities.

A Heart to Serve

The LORD is gracious and compassionate,
slow to anger and rich in love.

PSALM 145:8

*L*ord, I pray for a spirit of compassion. Help me to care about the needs of others and have genuine love for the ones I serve. Pour into me Your caring, kind Spirit, so I can be a blessing and minister out of a full heart. Fill me to overflowing so my ministry will be effective, growing, and blessed. May I walk in Your graciousness with a heart to serve.

Protection and Safety

The LORD will protect him and preserve his life; he will bless him in the land and not surrender him to the desire of his foes.

PSALM 41:2

*L*ord, You are my strength—please protect me. You are my safety—preserve me. Keep me safe in Your tender care as I minister to the needs of others. And please protect those around me, the ones to whom I minister. Bless me, Lord, and keep me from my enemies—the ones I see and the ones I don't. I ask for a strong wall of protection to keep out evil and keep in good. I trust You, my strong and mighty Lord.

Provision and Resources

❧

The next day we landed at Sidon; and Julius, in kindness to Paul, allowed him to go to his friends so they might provide for his needs.

ACTS 27:3

*L*ord, Your resources are unlimited. You delight to give Your children good gifts, to meet their needs. I boldly and humbly ask that You would provide for the needs of my ministry. Bring our ministry to the minds of people who are willing to give out of their God-given resources. May they give of their time, money, talents, or other resources to bless these ministry efforts to further Your kingdom.

Leadership

*If it is encouraging, let him encourage;
if it is contributing to the needs of others,
let him give generously; if it is leadership,
let him govern diligently; if it is showing
mercy, let him do it cheerfully.*

ROMANS 12:8

Lord, teach me Your ways. Show me how to be a leader who is first a servant. You showed us servant leadership when You washed the feet of Your disciples. Humble I come, Lord—let me be more like You. Deal with my pride and sin and selfishness, and help me to serve others with the right motives. Help me to be diligent in my tasks and encouraging in my words. Let me lead, Lord, with love.

Raise Up Volunteers

When he saw the crowds, he had compassion on them, because they were harassed and helpless, like sheep without a shepherd. Then he said to his disciples, "The harvest is plentiful but the workers are few. Ask the Lord of the harvest, therefore, to send out workers into his harvest field."

MATTHEW 9:36–38

*L*ord, the world is our mission field. From the nursery at church to the orphanages across the sea, there are children who need love and attention. From the streets of Columbus to the slums of Calcutta, people need to hear the Good News. The harvest is plentiful, and the workers are few—but I ask You, Lord of the harvest, to bring out people with hearts to serve. May they help my ministry and others in our nation and around the world.

Doing Greater Works

———————— ◎ ————————

"I tell you the truth, anyone who has faith in me will do what I have been doing. He will do even greater things than these, because I am going to the Father. And I will do whatever you ask in my name, so that the Son may bring glory to the Father."

JOHN 14:12–13

*L*ord, You are so amazing. You said we would do even greater things than You accomplished while on earth. I pray for great faith, that I may be a part of doing Your greater works. You healed the sick, made the lame walk, and radically changed Your generation. Empower me to help and heal in whatever way You call me to. May it delight You to answer my prayers and bring glory to Yourself.

Power of the Holy Spirit

Our gospel came to you not simply with words, but also with power, with the Holy Spirit and with deep conviction.

1 THESSALONIANS 1:5

Lord, in my own human effort I cannot make this ministry happen. I am totally dependent on You. I ask and pray for the power of Your Holy Spirit to fill me and work through me. Jump-start the compassion and conviction in my heart to minister life to others. Recharge me in my spirit and body to serve You effectively and well.

MY FRIENDS

The Power of Connection

Thank You for My Friendships

———— ❧ ————

A man of many companions may come to ruin, but there is a friend who sticks closer than a brother.

Proverbs 18:24

*L*ord, I thank You for my wonderful friends! As I think about the treasure chest of my close friends, casual friends, and acquaintances, I am grateful for the blessings and the joys each one brings to my life. Thank You for my "heart" friends, my loyal sister friends who listen, care, and encourage me. They are my faithful companions. I acknowledge that You, Lord, are the Giver of all good gifts, and I thank You for Your provision in my friendships.

A Deeper Walk
with God

I keep asking that the God of our Lord Jesus Christ, the glorious Father, may give you the Spirit of wisdom and revelation, so that you may know him better. I pray also that the eyes of your heart may be enlightened in order that you may know the hope to which he has called you, the riches of his glorious inheritance in the saints, and his incomparably great power for us who believe.

EPHESIANS 1:17–19

*L*ord, I ask in Jesus' name that my unsaved friend would come to know You as her personal Savior. I pray for her salvation and for her growth in faith. As You reveal Yourself to her, may she come to truly experience You—not just in her head but in her heart. Draw her closer to You, Lord, so she may feel the power of Your presence. Revive her spirit, Lord, for her sake and Your glory.

Friends Love Each Other

A friend loves at all times,
and a brother is born for adversity.

Proverbs 17:17

*L*ord, help me to be a friend who
loves at all times, even when I
may not feel like it. Teach me how to
love with words—to be encouraging and
supportive—and help me to show love
by my actions, too. I want to be a better
listener, never self-centered. Show me
how to bring joy to others in tangible
ways, with a phone call, a hug, or a deed
that is meaningful to my friend.

Jesus Is Your Friend

"Greater love has no one than this, that he lay down his life for his friends. You are my friends if you do what I command. I no longer call you servants, because a servant does not know his master's business. Instead, I have called you friends, for everything that I learned from my Father I have made known to you."

JOHN 15:13–15

Lord, You are my best friend. How could it be anyone else! You are kind, loving, generous, faithful, and giving. You always listen, and You always care. And You have the best advice. But most of all, You laid down Your life for me—for *me*, Lord! There is no greater expression of love, and for that I am immensely grateful. Thank You for calling me Your friend. Help me to learn Your ways so I can be a better friend to others.

Dealing with Enemies

Do not repay anyone evil for evil. Be careful to do what is right in the eyes of everybody. If it is possible, as far as it depends on you, live at peace with everyone. Do not take revenge, my friends, but leave room for God's wrath, for it is written: "It is mine to avenge; I will repay," says the Lord. On the contrary: "If your enemy is hungry, feed him; if he is thirsty, give him something to drink. In doing this, you will heap burning coals on his head." Do not be overcome by evil, but overcome evil with good.

ROMANS 12:17–21

Lord, I need wisdom in dealing with my adversaries. Teach me Your ways of justice, and help me to do what is right. I will not repay anyone evil for evil. I will not take it into my own hands, but I will allow You to avenge. I ask that You would bring good results from the iniquity of this situation. Give me the grace to leave it to You to make things right again. Please grant me the strength to live in peace.

When I Don't Know
What to Pray

In the same way, the Spirit helps us in our weakness. We do not know what we ought to pray for, but the Spirit himself intercedes for us with groans that words cannot express. And he who searches our hearts knows the mind of the Spirit, because the Spirit intercedes for the saints in accordance with God's will.

ROMANS 8:26–27

Lord, You know my friend's needs and the desires of her heart. But sometimes I don't know what to say or how to pray. Holy Spirit, You are the One who helps us in our weakness. When I do not know what to pray for, You intercede for me with groans that words cannot express. Search my heart and intercede for my friend today, Lord. I pray that Your will would be done.

Restoring a Broken Friendship

*Above all, love each other deeply, because
love covers over a multitude of sins.*

1 PETER 4:8

*L*ord, I thank You for Your healing
balm that covers the hurt and
pain I've experienced in this friendship.
Your grace covers me. Your love repairs
my brokenness, and You give me the
ability to love again. Help me to put
aside the wounds of my heart and to be a
friend again. I thank You and praise You
that Your love is healing and restoring.
Thank You, Lord, for putting this friendship back together.

Friends Help
Each Other

If one falls down, his friend can help him up.
But pity the man who falls and
has no one to help him up!

ECCLESIASTES 4:10

*L*ord, sometimes it's easier to give than to receive. I want to be a giver, to take the time to care and help my friends when they need it. And help me to learn to receive, too—so that I'm not too proud to receive generosity from a friend. Give and take, Lord. . . . We really do need each other.

MY EXTENDED FAMILY

*The Power of
Persistence*

Wisdom for
Daily Living

───── ◡ ─────

*Blessed is the man who finds wisdom,
the man who gains understanding,
for she is more profitable than silver
and yields better returns than gold.*

PROVERBS 3:13–14

*L*ord, I ask that my extended family members will know and experience Your wisdom each day. May they find that wisdom is more precious than rubies and that godly understanding is better than gold. Nothing they desire on earth can compare with knowing You and following Your ways. Some of them are far from You, Lord. I pray they would learn the ways of Your wisdom, the pleasantness of Your paths, and the peace that You bring.

Unconditional Love

"If you love those who love you, what reward will you get? Are not even the tax collectors doing that?"

Matthew 5:46

*L*ord, I thank You for my family members and those who are like family to me. I am grateful for their love and understanding. May I be loving in return—not only with those who love me but even with those who are hard to be around. Your ways are merciful and kind, forgiving and good. Help me to reflect Your love, finding joy in loving others as You love me.

Living in Peace and Harmony

⟳

Rejoice with those who rejoice; mourn with those who mourn. Live in harmony with one another. Do not be proud, but be willing to associate with people of low position. Do not be conceited.

Romans 12:15–16

Lord, I want to be a person of peace and live in harmony with others. I know that my family members and I don't always agree. But when we disagree, help us to work through our differences and connect again with each other. Please give me empathy, allowing me to rejoice with those who rejoice and mourn with those who mourn. Make me open, Lord, to associating with people regardless of their status or position.

Don't Gossip

*A gossip betrays a confidence,
but a trustworthy man keeps a secret.*

PROVERBS 11:13

*L*ord, sometimes it's such a temptation to talk about other people. I like to be "in the know," but I don't want my listening and sharing to become gossip. Show me the line between relating needed information and gossiping—passing along rumors that may hurt a friend or family member. Help me to be a woman who can keep a secret and not betray a confidence. Help me to be trustworthy in all my conversations, Lord.

Healing for Envy
and Jealousy

---

*A heart at peace gives life to the body,
but envy rots the bones.*

PROVERBS 14:30

*L*ord, I'm feeling envious—and I
need Your help. It's hard to keep
my feelings in check when I want what
someone else has. Wherever I look, Lord,
I see people who have something more
or better than I do, and that makes me
struggle inside. I have longings, Lord, but
I want a heart at peace. Take away this
envy and jealousy, and help me to be content, knowing that You will provide for all
my needs. I choose to trust You, Lord.

Being a Blessing
to Others

Love must be sincere. Hate what is evil;
cling to what is good. Be devoted to one
another in brotherly love. Honor one
another above yourselves.

ROMANS 12:9–10

Lord, I want to be a blessing to my extended family. I will pray for the ones You bring to mind—those who need prayer most. I bless all of them, Lord, whether I know them well or not, because You love them. Help me to be sincere in honoring them. I pray for their needs, their salvation, and their healing. I pray also that they would learn to know and enjoy You.

Praying for the Generations

O my people, hear my teaching; listen to the words of my mouth. I will open my mouth in parables, I will utter hidden things, things from of old—what we have heard and known, what our fathers have told us. We will not hide them from their children; we will tell the next generation the praiseworthy deeds of the LORD, his power, and the wonders he has done.

PSALM 78:1–4

Lord, I pray for the people who will come after me—my children, grandchildren, and great-grandchildren, and even those who come after that. May they love and serve You, Lord, and make a difference for good in their generation. Open my mouth to speak of Your wonders, Your power, and Your love to my family so the next generations will know and honor You.

Praying for One Another

They all joined together constantly in prayer, along with the women and Mary the mother of Jesus, and with his brothers.

ACTS 1:14

Lord, teach me to pray. And please help our family members to pray for each other. May we be focused, fervent, and faithful in coming boldly before You. Stir within each of us how best to pray for one another. Help us to develop oneness as we intercede. Give us wisdom and grace to love each other more consistently. Revive our family life for Your good purposes and Your glory.

MY NATION

The Power of Respect for Authority

God Bless America

———— ๑ ————

Give thanks to the LORD, call on his name;
make known among the nations
what he has done.

PSALM 105:1

I praise You, Lord, thanking You for this great nation. You have blessed America! Thank You for peace. Thank You for the freedom to speak and be heard and to vote for our leaders. We are a nation of diverse and independent people, Lord, and I pray we would respect each other. Help us to uphold godly values as we seek to honor the authority of those who govern our land. Please keep the United States united— as one strong country that seeks Your face and favor.

Respect for Authority

Consequently, he who rebels against the authority is rebelling against what God has instituted, and those who do so will bring judgment on themselves. For rulers hold no terror for those who do right, but for those who do wrong. Do you want to be free from fear of the one in authority? Then do what is right and he will commend you.

ROMANS 13:2–3

*L*ord, I pray for the men and women who hold influence and power in our nation. From police officers to Supreme Court justices, give them the conscience to do what is right—even when right and wrong seem interchangeable these days. I pray that our leaders would maintain credibility so we as American people can honor and respect them. Please help us to train our children to respect authority, as well. I pray for the integrity and morality of all who have authority in our republic, Lord.

Praying for National Leaders

I urge, then, first of all, that requests, prayers, intercession and thanksgiving be made for everyone—for kings and all those in authority, that we may live peaceful and quiet lives in all godliness and holiness.

1 TIMOTHY 2:1–2

*L*ord, I pray for our nation's leaders and ask that You would give them the ability to make wise decisions, to govern with integrity, and to accomplish their tasks in ways that build up our nation. May all the people I pray for now bring glory and honor to Your name as they serve our country: the president; the vice president; the secretaries of state, defense, homeland security, the interior, the treasury, agriculture, commerce, labor, transportation, energy, education, veterans affairs, health and human services, and housing and urban development; the attorney general; the national security advisor; the director of national intelligence; and the Supreme Court justices.

Praying for State Leaders

*Wisdom makes one wise man more
powerful than ten rulers in a city.*

ECCLESIASTES 7:19

*L*ord, I pray for the men and
women in our state government—
that they will make good policy in humility and godly wisdom. Bless their lives as
they balance their work and families. Give
them the strength and integrity to govern
wisely. May all the people I pray for now
be faithful stewards of their office and
serve the people of our state for the glory
of God's name: our state representatives
and senators, our governor, and our state
Supreme Court justices.

Praying for Local Leaders

The prayer of a righteous man is powerful and effective.

JAMES 5:16

*L*ord, I pray that the leaders in our city and local area would lead with integrity, honesty, and fairness. May they be hungry for Your power, not for temporary control over others. May all the people I pray for now lead with justice, grace, and mercy as they serve our community for Your glory: our mayor, our judges and court officials, members of the police and fire departments, and other civic leaders.

Praying for the Armed Forces

The LORD is my strength and my shield; my heart trusts in him, and I am helped.

PSALM 28:7

*L*ord, I thank You for all the men and women serving in our armed forces. They choose to put their lives on the line so we can have freedom and peace—and for that I am truly grateful. I ask that You would bless them for their loyalty and service. Protect them and keep them safe. Comfort them and give them strength when they are away from loved ones. Bless, too, the families who send soldiers to war or for duty overseas. I pray that You would meet their every need, Lord.

Blessings for Obedience

If you fully obey the LORD your God and carefully follow all his commands I give you today, the LORD your God will set you high above all the nations on earth. All these blessings will come upon you and accompany you if you obey the LORD your God: You will be blessed in the city and blessed in the country. The fruit of your womb will be blessed, and the crops of your land and the young of your livestock—the calves of your herds and the lambs of your flocks. Your basket and your kneading trough will be blessed. You will be blessed when you come in and blessed when you go out.

DEUTERONOMY 28:1–6

Lord, I humbly bow before You and thank You for the power to obey and follow Your ways. Your Word tells us that obedience leads to blessings. I don't want to miss my blessings. I don't want my family or friends—or anyone else—to miss the best in their lives either. So I ask for forgiveness when I have done wrong and strength to make better choices. Help all of us to walk in faithfulness, empowered by Your Holy Spirit.

Spiritual Revival in America

"Abraham will surely become a great and powerful nation, and all nations on earth will be blessed through him."

GENESIS 18:18

Revive us, O Lord! I pray for a great awakening of hope, healing, and salvation in America. Forgive us our personal sins and the sins of our people. May our nation fulfill her great destiny and purposes. Awaken us to our need for You and our total dependence on You. Bless us, Lord, to be a nation that is powerful—so we can be strong within and a blessing to the other nations on earth.

MY DREAMS
AND GOALS

The Power of Surrender

Daring to Dream

———————— ☺ ————————

Delight yourself in the LORD and he
will give you the desires of your heart.

PSALM 37:4

Dear Giver of dreams, I believe
You've placed dreams within me
that are yet to be realized. Teach me to
delight myself in You as I pursue the desires of my heart. Show me Your perfect
will—may I move as far and as fast as
you wish, never less or more. Grant me
the wisdom I need to accomplish Your
plans for my life and the humility to
give You the glory in them.

Knowing God's Will

Do not conform any longer to the pattern of this world, but be transformed by the renewing of your mind. Then you will be able to test and approve what God's will is—his good, pleasing and perfect will.

ROMANS 12:2

*L*ord, I commit my aspirations to You. Give me the courage to work toward my own goals and not be swayed by the opinions of others. Renew my mind and my spirit so I will be able to test and approve what Your will is—Your good, pleasing, and perfect will. I don't have to be afraid that I will miss it—I can know that You bring people and circumstances into my life for a reason. Thank You for the assurance that You will direct me into Your good purposes.

Trusting God's Wisdom

For the LORD gives wisdom, and from his mouth come knowledge and understanding.

PROVERBS 2:6

*L*ord, what a blessing it is to be able to come before You—the wisest, most intelligent Being in the universe. I have direct access straight to the top. Thank You for giving me wisdom and direction, even when I can't see the way. Knowledge and understanding come directly from Your mouth, Lord, and You delight to enlighten us. I praise You and ask for continued insight as my dreams become achievable goals.

Nothing Is Too Hard for God

"I am the LORD, the God of all mankind. Is anything too hard for me?"

JEREMIAH 32:27

*L*ord, I want things to be different in my life—but there are so many obstacles. I need energy and motivation to get going. I need finances and more time. More than anything, I need to trust You more. Nothing is too difficult for You, Father. You can do anything! Despite all my needs and distractions, please bring into my life favor and openings— please make a way. I ask that You would help me achieve the goals in my life that are best suited for Your good purposes.

Being a Woman of Action

In the same way, faith by itself, if it is not accompanied by action, is dead.

JAMES 2:17

*L*ord, I want to be a woman of action—a woman of true faith. Faith by itself—if only thoughts and words—is dead. It has to be accompanied by my deeds, Lord. I pray for the wisdom to know when to take risks, when to act, and when to wait. Help me to know the right thing to do and the best time to do it. Put true faith into me, Lord, so I can perform the good works You have for me to accomplish.

God Is Faithful

The one who calls you is
faithful and he will do it.

1 THESSALONIANS 5:24

Lord, I thank You that You are my faithful God. No one else is like You. People move away, jobs change, and much of life is uncertain. But You are always here, my stable, loving, and present Lord. Help me to hold unswervingly to the hope I profess, for You alone are faithful. You keep all Your promises—every one of them, all the time—and I thank You for that, Lord.

Surrendering Your Dreams

Going a little farther, he fell with his face to the ground and prayed, "My Father, if it is possible, may this cup be taken from me. Yet not as I will, but as you will."

MATTHEW 26:39

*L*ord, I humbly bow before You and give You my dreams. I give up control. I surrender my will for Yours. When I am tempted to do things my way, may I seek Your guidance instead. When I am too pushy, trying to make things happen on my own, give me patience to see that Your grace has everything covered. I don't have to be afraid, Lord. I will trust You to meet my every need.

Holding on to Hope

Against all hope, Abraham in hope believed
and so became the father of many nations,
just as it had been said to him, "So
shall your offspring be."

ROMANS 4:18

*L*ord, please help me hold on to
hope. Sustain me according to
Your promises. Abraham had great faith
in You, Lord, and became the father of
many nations—just as You had prom-
ised him. Even though he was old, You
provided a baby boy for him and his
wife, Sarah. As You did for them, Lord,
please fulfill my longings—and Your
vision for my life's purpose.

MY PERSONAL HISTORY

The Power of Transformation

Returning to the Lord

⊘

Rend your heart and not your garments.
Return to the LORD your God, for he is
gracious and compassionate, slow to anger
and abounding in love, and he relents
from sending calamity.

JOEL 2:13

*L*ord, some of the things in my
past have led me far from You. I
want to come back and be in right standing with You again. I ask for forgiveness
for the things I have done wrong—in
both my distant past and more recently.
I am so glad that You are gracious and
compassionate. Thank You for being
slow to anger and abounding in love.
Here I am, Lord. I return to You.

Forgiving Others

"Do not judge, and you will not be judged. Do not condemn, and you will not be condemned. Forgive, and you will be forgiven."

LUKE 6:37

*L*ord, it can be so hard to forgive—especially when I feel that other people don't deserve it. But I don't deserve Your forgiveness either, and You freely forgive me when I ask. Because of Your great mercy toward me, help me to forgive the people who've hurt me in the past. Help me to know that forgiving is not condoning—but it releases me to Your freedom. I leave the retribution to You, God of justice and love.

We Need to Remember

And Joshua set up at Gilgal the twelve stones they had taken out of the Jordan. He said to the Israelites, "In the future when your descendants ask their fathers, 'What do these stones mean?' tell them, 'Israel crossed the Jordan on dry ground.' For the LORD your God dried up the Jordan before you until you had crossed over. The LORD your God did to the Jordan just what he had done to the Red Sea when he dried it up before us until we had crossed over."

JOSHUA 4:20–23

*L*ord, I want to remember the good things You have done for me in the past. Like the stones the Israelites took out of the Jordan River, I need my own personal "rocks of remembrance" of Your mercies in my life. You performed miracles for them—allowing them to cross the river on dry ground, parting the Red Sea for them—so that people today might know Your powerful hand. As I recall the ways You have helped me throughout my life, I honor You.

We Need to Forget

Not that I have already obtained all this, or have already been made perfect, but I press on to take hold of that for which Christ Jesus took hold of me. Brothers, I do not consider myself yet to have taken hold of it. But one thing I do: Forgetting what is behind and straining toward what is ahead, I press on toward the goal to win the prize for which God has called me heavenward in Christ Jesus.

PHILIPPIANS 3:12–14

*L*ord, help me forget the things in my past that I need to leave behind. Give me the courage to press on. There is a goal waiting for me, a reward in heaven—and I want to win the prize! You, Jesus, were always going about Your Father's business. Help me to face forward and move on, marching boldly into the future. I may not know what will happen from here, but I know the One who does.

Learning from the Past

———— 🌀 ————

Not only so, but we also rejoice in our
sufferings, because we know that suffering
produces perseverance; perseverance,
character; and character, hope.

ROMANS 5:3–4

*L*ord, I thank You for Your
patience as I learn important
lessons from my past. I don't want to
repeat my mistakes, Lord. Your ways are
not our ways, but Your ways are best.
They bring healing and life. As I learn
to rejoice in the suffering I've experienced, I can see Your hand teaching
me perseverance; from perseverance I
develop character, and from character I
have hope.

Living in the Present

Come, let us bow down in worship, let us kneel before the LORD our Maker; for he is our God and we are the people of his pasture, the flock under his care. Today, if you hear his voice, do not harden your hearts.

PSALM 95:6–8

*L*ord, I have been camping in the past too long. Pull up my tent stakes, and help me to move on. There is so much to live for today! The past is over, and the future awaits. Today I choose to worship You, my Lord and Maker. When I hear Your voice, may my heart be soft—not hardened or jaded by the past. Today is a gift; I celebrate the present with You, Lord.

Change Me, Lord

Yet, O LORD, you are our Father.
We are the clay, you are the potter;
we are all the work of your hand.

ISAIAH 64:8

*L*ord, You know all about me—my past, my present, and my future. You are the potter, and I am the clay, the work of Your hands. As You reshape my life, changing me from who I was and molding me into the woman You want me to be, help me to trust Your wisdom. I want to be a vessel sturdy enough to hold all the love You have for me—and to pour that love out on others.

All Things Work Together for Good

And we know that in all things God works for the good of those who love him, who have been called according to his purpose.

ROMANS 8:28

*L*ord, sometimes it's hard to understand why things had to happen the way they did. I have made some poor choices, but other people have done some really hurtful things to me, too. Even though I may never completely understand, I trust that You work things out for the good, for Your own glory. I love You, Lord, and I know I have been called according to Your purpose. I will put my faith in You.

MY INNER LIFE

The Power of
Christ-Centered Living

Living a Life of Love

---

*"And the second is like it:
'Love your neighbor as yourself.'"*

MATTHEW 22:39

ord, I want to live a life of love! Show me what true love is— Your love—so I can receive it and give it away to others. Teach me to care for my neighbor as I would care for myself. Let love be my motivation for action. Help me to speak kind, encouraging words and to bless others with my actions as well. I thank You that Your amazing, unconditional, accepting love sustains me.

Personal Revival

*May our Lord Jesus Christ himself and God
our Father, who loved us and by his grace
gave us eternal encouragement and good hope,
encourage your hearts and strengthen
you in every good deed and word.*

2 THESSALONIANS 2:16–17

*L*ord, I have neglected time with
You, and I am sorry. Please
forgive me. Blow a fresh wind into the
staleness of my life, and revive my spirit.
Help me put aside my selfishness and
seek You first. Awaken my soul to the
goodness of Your love, for You are my
heart's desire. Away from the clamor of
television and traffic, I come into Your
stillness. Thank You for causing me to
linger and enjoy Your refreshment, joy,
and peace.

Cleanse My Heart

*If we confess our sins, he is faithful and
just and will forgive us our sins and
purify us from all unrighteousness.*

1 JOHN 1:9

*L*ord, I humbly ask for forgiveness of sin in my life. I repent and turn from doing wrong things. I don't know why I do the things I don't want to do. Sometimes it's willful, and sometimes I'm just careless. Thank You for Your loving-kindness and mercy that cleanse my soul and let me be in right standing with You again. Cleanse me, heal me, and make me whole, Lord.

Empower My Life

"If you then, though you are evil, know how to give good gifts to your children, how much more will your Father in heaven give the Holy Spirit to those who ask him!"

LUKE 11:13

Holy Spirit, I cannot live life on my own strength. I ask that You would come and fill me with Your presence. Empower me with discernment to make better life choices and energy to thrive—not just survive. Give me a heart to seek You and serve others. Pour into my life more love, joy, peace, and patience—to be a caring mom, a loving wife, a good friend, a wise worker— make me a woman who is blessed, Lord.

Knowing Your Worth and Value

"Are not two sparrows sold for a penny?
Yet not one of them will fall to the ground
apart from the will of your Father. . . .
So don't be afraid; you are worth
more than many sparrows."

MATTHEW 10:29, 31

Lord, I have sought to find my significance in places other than Your heart. Forgive me for putting weight in what other people think or in my own efforts. I thank You that You value me because I am Your child—and that I have great worth no matter what I look like or do for a living. You find the unfading beauty of a gentle and quiet spirit to be of great worth in Your sight. Thank You for loving and valuing me, Lord.

Beautiful Inside and Out

But the LORD said to Samuel, "Do not consider his appearance or his height, for I have rejected him. The LORD does not look at the things man looks at. Man looks at the outward appearance, but the LORD looks at the heart."

1 SAMUEL 16:7

Lord, our world is so focused on outward appearance—nice clothes and good looks. But You're never like that. People may look at the hairstyles and the outfits, but You look at the heart. Lord, please help me to work with what You've given me on the outside—as I also polish my inner character. May Your beauty shine through me as I praise You more and more. Be my light within that I may radiate the love of Christ.

A Woman of Wisdom

*Blessed is the man who finds wisdom,
the man who gains understanding,
for she is more profitable than silver
and yields better returns than gold.*

PROVERBS 3:13–14

*L*ord, I want to be a woman of wisdom, not foolishness. Help me to make right choices and conduct myself in a manner worthy of Your name. I pray that I would be honest and upright in my daily life so my actions reflect who You are. Help me to act with integrity, so I become a person who keeps her promises and commitments.

A Thankful Heart

Be joyful always; pray continually;
give thanks in all circumstances, for this
is God's will for you in Christ Jesus.

1 Thessalonians 5:16–18

*L*ord, You are my God—and it is
my joy to give You my inner heart.
Cleanse me, fill me, heal me, and help
me to live with a joyful, thankful heart.
I want to be a woman of prayer. I want
to make a difference in my world. For all
You are and all You do, I am grateful. I
give You praise for the blessings in my life.

MY FUTURE

The Power of Hope

A Bedrock of Faith

So that your faith might not rest on men's wisdom, but on God's power.

1 CORINTHIANS 2:5

*L*ord, please set me firmly on a bedrock of faith so that my decisions will rest solidly on You—not the wisdom of humans or my own fickle feelings. Strong and secure, Lord, You are my foundation. Build in me hope and faith as I put my trust in You. No matter what may happen—or what may threaten—please let my life stand firm through trials. Establish the work of Your hands, Lord, rock solid in me.

Always Have Hope

*We have this hope as an anchor for the soul,
firm and secure.*

HEBREWS 6:19

*L*ord, please help me look forward
with a positive attitude—with
faith, not fear. Anchor me with hope
for my soul, firm and secure. Captain
the craft of my life, and keep me from
wandering into doubt and insecurity
over the future. I thank You, Lord, that
You are in control!

Live Powerfully

*Grow in the grace and knowledge of our
Lord and Savior Jesus Christ. To him
be glory both now and forever!*

2 PETER 3:18

ord, You have all power and authority. You are the highest ruler in the land—in the entire universe! What a privilege it is to come humbly yet boldly before You and ask You to empower me today. For all I need to do, for all I need to say, may Your favor rest on me. May Your blessings, Lord, flow through my life—and may I also be a blessing to others.

Walking in Wisdom

A man's own folly ruins his life,
yet his heart rages against the LORD.

PROVERBS 19:3

Lord, please keep me from the foolishness of sin. I ask for wisdom and discernment to make wise choices in my life. When I'm tempted, give me the strength to flee it. When I am uncertain, help me to know the right course of action. When I need good ideas, enlighten my mind with creativity and intelligence. You know everything, Lord—may I walk in Your wisdom and learn Your ways.

God Finishes
What He Starts

*Being confident of this, that he who began
a good work in you will carry it on to
completion until the day of Christ Jesus.*

PHILIPPIANS 1:6

*L*ord, I am so glad You finish
what You start in us. You get the
job done—and I'm grateful for that.
You don't leave us like an unfinished
project on a workbench. You don't get
distracted and forget. Thank You, Lord!
You have started my life, and I know
You will finish the development of my
character for Your good purpose in my
life. Create in me integrity, faith, and
joy, Lord, and help me to finish well.

My Times Are
in God's Hands

*But I trust in you, O LORD; I say,
"You are my God." My times are in
your hands; deliver me from my enemies
and from those who pursue me.*

PSALM 31:14–15

*L*ord, I thank You that Your hands
are strong and steady. My times
are in Your hands—and that's a good
place for them to be. In my hands they
could fall and break. But not in Yours.
Your hands create, Your hands guide and
direct, and Your hands hold and comfort. I am secure in every season of my
life, knowing that You will protect me
and keep me safe. Hand in hand, may
we face the future with hope.

God Has Good
Plans for Me

———— ⟲ ————

"For I know the plans I have for you,"
*declares the L*ORD, *"plans to prosper you*
and not to harm you, plans to give you hope
and a future. Then you will call upon me and
come and pray to me, and I will listen to you.
You will seek me and find me when you
seek me with all your heart."

JEREMIAH 29:11–13

*L*ord, I am glad to know that You
have plans for me—because the
future is so unclear in my mind. You
desire to prosper, not to harm me. As
the Giver of all good gifts, You wrap
up hope and a future as my present.
I call upon You, Lord, knowing that
You always listen. I seek You with all
my heart, Lord, and look forward with
expectant hope to good things to come.

Peace

Do not be anxious about anything, but in everything, by prayer and petition, with thanksgiving, present your requests to God. And the peace of God, which transcends all understanding, will guard your hearts and your minds in Christ Jesus.

PHILIPPIANS 4:6–7

Lord, You are my peace. Amid life's uncertainties, chaos, and sorrows, I do not have to be anxious. In everything, I will pray and ask for Your help, guidance, and direction. I give You my challenges and present You my needs. I thank You for Your settling peace, which transcends all understanding. May Your serenity calm my heart and guard my mind in Christ Jesus.

Joy

*The LORD is my strength and my shield;
my heart trusts in him, and I am helped.
My heart leaps for joy and I will give
thanks to him in song.*

*L*ord, You are my joy. Knowing You gives me gladness and
strength. As my heart's shield, You
protect me from harm. Help me to face
the future with joy. Fill me with Your
pleasures so I may bring enjoyment to
my surroundings—at home, at work,
and in my ministry. Help me to laugh
more and smile often as I reflect on
Your goodness. In Your presence, Lord,
is fullness of joy.

CONCLUSION
The Power of Prayer

❋

*"I am the vine; you are the branches.
If a man remains in me and I in him,
he will bear much fruit; apart from
me you can do nothing."*

JOHN 15:5

Just as fruit trees bear a variety of crops—apples, peaches, cherries— each of us will bear different kinds of fruit, the blessings in our lives. The abundant harvest could be an encouraged friend, a stronger marriage, healthy kids, or a heart at peace. For some the harvest will be unseen fruit, a forthcoming abundance that will be gathered and enjoyed by future generations because of your faithful prayers today. In their various shapes and forms, our prayers and God's provision create a cornucopia of His blessings and grace.

Getting connected and staying connected help us to pray powerfully. Keep on praying with courage and tenacity. Never give up. Women who pray are women who love well, live victoriously, and make a difference in the world. My hope is that you will be one of them.